write math answers to

f

open–ended questions
in algebra

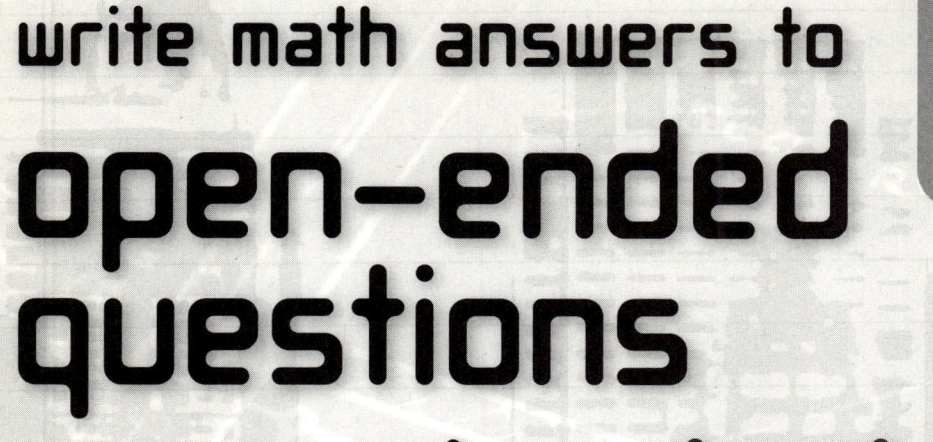

think... oranges 4 x $0
apples 6 x $0.45
plums 3n

$(4 \times \$0.75) + (6 \times \$0.45) + (\$3n)$
$(\$3.00) + (\$2.70) + (\$3n)$
$\$5.70 + \$3n$

To find the total cost of the fruit purchased, I added the costs of the oranges, apples, and plums. The oranges cost 4 x $0.75. The apples cost 6 x $0.45. Because the cost of plums changes from day to day, let n be the unknown cost of plums. The cost of plums is $3 \times n = 3n$. So, the total cost of the fruit can be found by solving the expression $(4 \times \$0.75) + (6 \times \$0.45) + (\$3n)$. I simplified the expression to get the answers $\$5.70 + \$3n$.

New Readers Press

Write Math Answers to Open-Ended Questions in Algebra Level F
ISBN 978-1-56420-801-9

Printed in the United States of America
9 8 7 6 5 4 3 2 1

All proceeds from the sale of New Readers Press materials
support literacy programs in the United States and worldwide.

Developer: Words & Numbers
Developmental Editor: Terrie Lipke
Creative Director: Andrea Woodbury
Production Specialist: Maryellen Casey

contents

1 addition and

sigr

A **signed number** is either positive or negative. For example, +4 and –2 are signed numbers. Positive numbers are usually written without a sign. So, +4 is written as 4. The absolute value of any signed number is positive. | 4 | = 4 and | –2 | = 2.

problem: Karly and Li are playing a game. They draw cards and follow the instructions on the cards by moving their game pieces on a number line. Karly's game piece is on 2 and Li's game piece is on –1.

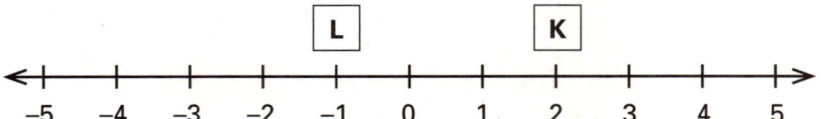

a. Karly draws a card that reads "Add –3." Write a number sentence that shows how Karly can move her piece and where it will land. Explain in words how you found your answer.

b. Li draws a card that reads "Subtract –5." Write a number sentence that shows how Li can move her piece and where it will land. Explain in words how you found your answer.

understand
the problem

Where are the game pieces now? _____

What instructions do the players have to follow? _____

_____

What is a number sentence? _____

_____

think
it through

a. Karly's number sentence will look like this:
starting number + number on card = ending number
    2   +   –3   = ending number
Karly needs to add numbers that have different signs.

| 2 | = _____ | –3 | = _____   3 – 2 = _____

Use the sign of –3 for the sum. The sum is –1.

Remember:
Subtract the absolute values and keep the sign of the number with the greater absolute value.

answer
the question

Karly's number sentence is: _____ + _____ = _____.

explain
your answer

To explain your answer, describe how you add the numbers on a number line.

Karly needs to add −3, so she will move _____ spaces to the _____.

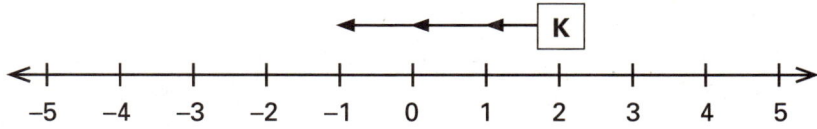

When Karly starts at 2 and adds −3, she ends on −1.

The number sentence $2 + -3 = -1$ describes Karly's move.

think
it through

b. Li's number sentence will have this form:

starting number − _____ = _____

To find where Li will land, find $-1 - (-5)$, or $-1 +$ _____.

> **Remember:**
> **To subtract a negative**
> **number, add its**
> **opposite.**

answer
the question

Li's number sentence is: _____ − _____ = _____

explain
your answer

To find out where Li's piece will land, I subtracted on a number line. Li needs to subtract _____, so she will move _____ spaces to the _____.

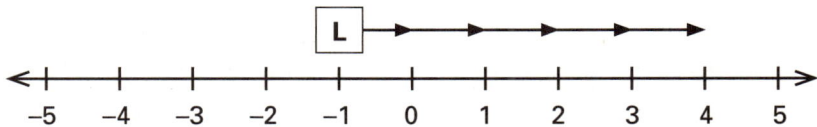

When Li starts at −1 and subtracts −5, she lands on 4. The number sentence $-1 - (-5) = 4$ describes Li's move.

1. Carl and Daniel are playing the number line game. Daniel's game piece is on 2. He draws a card that reads "Subtract –4."

    a. Write a number sentence that shows how Daniel can follow his instruction and where he will land.

    b. Draw a number line and use it to explain how you got your answer. Show the starting point, how the game piece is moved, and the ending point.

2. Carl's game piece is on –1. He draws a card with an "add" instruction. He follows the instruction and lands on –6.

    a. What is the complete instruction on Carl's card? _____

    b. Write the number sentence that shows how Carl follows the instruction.

    c. Draw a number line to show how you found your answer.

3. At 10:00 P.M., the temperature was 1°C. In the next hour, the temperature decreased 3°C. In the next hour after that, the temperature decreased another 4°C.

a. Explain in words how you would find what the temperature was at midnight.

b. What was the temperature at midnight? Write a number sentence that shows how you found your answer.

Temperature at midnight _____

Number sentence _____

4. Elaine's family is scuba diving. Elaine is watching from the boat's lookout $4\frac{1}{2}$ feet above the surface of the water. Directly below Elaine, Tameka is exploring a coral reef 12 feet below the surface of the water.

a. Write a subtraction sentence that shows the distance between Elaine and Tameka. What is the distance? Explain how you found your answer.

b. Walt is swimming 4 feet directly below Tameka. Find the distance between Elaine and Walt. Write a number sentence and draw a diagram that shows how you found your answer.

2 multiplication and

sigr

The product or quotient of two numbers with the same sign is positive.
The product or quotient of two numbers with different signs is negative.

problem: Ravi is keeping track of temperatures. He records the temperature each morning for seven days. What is the average temperature for the week? Explain your answer.

Sun.	Mon.	Tues.	Wed.	Thurs.	Fri.	Sat.
2°C	–3°C	1°C	–6°C	2°C	–6°C	–4°C

understand
the problem

What do you need to find? _____

What information do you need to find it? _____

think
it through

How will you find the average temperature? _____

_____

How many readings are there? _____

What is the sum of the readings? _____

What is the average temperature? _____

answer
the question

The average temperature is _____.

Remember: Use units (°C) when writing your final answer.

explain
your answer

To find the average temperature, I first added the temperature readings from each morning to get a sum of _____. Next, I divided by the number of readings, which is 7. This gives me the average temperature, which is _____°C.

division with
2d numbers

> **problem:** Charlene made a pattern of numbers:
> –1, 3, –6, 18, –36, 108, ... Describe the rule for the pattern in
> words. Then, use the rule for the pattern to write the next term.

understand
the problem

What are the terms in the pattern? _____

think
it through

Find a rule that describes how to find each term by looking at the previous term.

Look at one term. Then, describe an operation you could use to find the next term.

Look for an addition pattern:

There is no addition pattern.

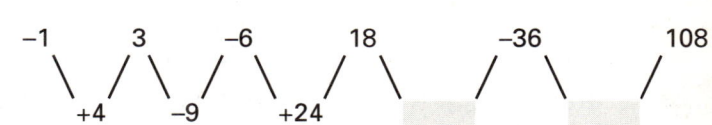

Look for a multiplication pattern: –1

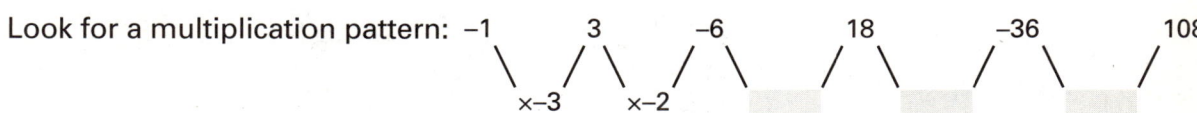

The pattern is _____

To find the next term in the pattern _____

_____ × _____ = _____

answer
the question

The rule for the pattern is _____

The next term in the pattern is _____

explain
your answer

The signs of the numbers in the pattern alternate between + and –, so a
_____ number is next. The factors of 2 and 3 alternate.
–36 × _____ = 108, so the next factor is _____. 108 × _____ = _____

1. Five days last week, Oscar recorded temperatures of 4°C, –3°C, –6°C, –7°C, and –3°C.

a. What is the average temperature for the five days? Show your work.

The average temperature was _____.

b. On the sixth day, the temperature was 3°C. What is the average temperature for the six days? Explain your answer.

The average temperature was _____.

2. A football team had possession of the ball for 8 plays during one quarter of a game. The results of the plays are shown in the table.

Play #1	Play #2	Play #3	Play #4	Play #5	Play #6	Play #7	Play #8
8 yard loss	3 yard gain	4 yard loss	6 yard loss	5 yard gain	no gain or loss	1 yard gain	27 yard loss

a. What signed number shows the average result for the 8 possessions? Show your work.

The signed number _____ shows the average result.

b. Was the average result a gain or loss of yards? Explain how you know.

The average result was a _____ of yards. I know

because _____ numbers represent gains, and

_____ numbers represent losses.

3. Nadia made the number pattern below.

$$1 \quad -4 \quad 2 \quad -8 \quad 4 \quad -16 \quad 8$$

a. What is the rule for the number pattern?

The rule for the number pattern is: _____

b. Use the rule to write the next two terms in the pattern. Explain your answer.

The next two terms are: _____

4. Multiplication is a way to show repeated addition of the same number. So, the expression $5 + 5 + 5$ can be written as 3×5.

a. Write an addition expression that is the same as 6×-4.5.

b. Explain how you can use a number line to check your answer for part a.

3 order of

ope

When evaluating expressions, you must perform the operations in order. First, evaluate expressions inside parentheses. Next, evaluate exponents. Then, multiply and divide from left to right. Finally, add and subtract from left to right.

problem: The expression $\frac{\$25 + (3 \times \$39)}{2}$ represents the amount of money Kim and her roommate Ann will each pay to have their kitchen painted. How much will each woman pay?

understand
the problem

What is the expression? _____

What operations appear in the expression? _____

think
it through

What operation will you complete first? _____

What operation will you complete next? _____

answer
the question

Simplify the expression by using the order of operations.

$= \dfrac{\$25 + (3 \times \$39)}{2}$

$= \dfrac{\$25 + ()}{2}$ ◀ Evaluate parentheses.

$= \dfrac{}{2}$ ◀ Simplify numerator.

$= $ ◀ Divide.

> Remember: The numerator acts as a group. Simplify the numerator before dividing.

Each woman will pay _____.

explain
your answer

I used the order of operations to find the value of the expression. The fraction bar is a grouping symbol, so I started with the operations in the numerator, and calculated inside the parentheses first. (3 x $39) = _____.
Then I added to get 25 + 117 = _____. Finally, I divided to find $\frac{142}{2}$ = $ _____.

...rations

> **problem**: To find the number of square inches of cardboard needed to make a box, Adrian used the expression $2 \times 4^2 + 4(2 \times 8)$. What is the area of cardboard Adrian needs? Show your work.

understand the problem

What operation is indicated when 4 is placed next to the parentheses in $4(2 \times 8)$?

_____

What units will your answer have? _____

think it through

In what order will you complete the operations? _____

_____

answer the question

Simplify the expression.

$2 \times 4^2 + 4(2 \times 8)$

$= 2 \times 4^2 + 4()$

$= 2 \times + 4()$

$= + $

$= $

Adrian needs _____ of cardboard to make the box.

> Remember:
> An exponent tells how many times to use the base as a factor.

explain your answer

I evaluated the operations in parentheses first. $(2 \times 8) =$ _____. After that, I checked for any exponents. There was one, so I calculated it: $4^2 =$ _____. Because I should multiply before adding, I multiplied $2 \times 16 =$ _____ and $4(16) =$ _____. Finally, I added: _____ $+ 64 =$ _____.

1. George used the expression $\frac{3^2 \times 2}{3} + 3^2 \times 4$ to find the total volume, in cubic inches, of a doghouse he built. What is the total volume of the doghouse? Explain your answer.

The volume of the doghouse is _____.

2. The expression $4(3.5) + 6(8)$ represents the total length, in inches, of yarn that Miranda will need to do a craft project. Simplify the expression to find the length of yarn Miranda needs. Show your work.

Miranda needs _____ of yarn.

3. **a.** How can you place parentheses in the expression $3 \times 8 + 4^2 - 8 \div 2$ so that the expression is equal to 28?

b. Show that the expression you made in part a is equal to 28. Describe your answer.

4. Mr. Nelson bought four drinks for $2 each and four snack packs for $7 each at the movies. He gave the cashier $40.

a. Write an expression using order of operations that can be used to find how much change Mr. Nelson will receive.

b. How much change will Mr. Nelson receive? Explain how you arrived at your answer.

Mr. Nelson received _____ in change.

4 variables and

exp

A **variable** is a letter used to represent an unknown number. You can use variables to write expressions that show operations on unknown numbers. For example, to add 3 to an unknown number *n,* write $n + 3$. To multiply an unknown number *p* by –4, write $-4p$.

problem: Michelle has 3 pencils. She purchased a few packages of pencils. Each package contained 10 pencils.

a. What variable expression can be used to show the total number of pencils Michelle has now? Use *p* as a variable.

b. Evaluate the expression if $p = 5$.

understand
the problem

What quantity is unknown? _____

How many pencils did Michelle have to start? _____

How many pencils were in each package? _____

Can you find the total number of pencils from the information in the problem? Why

or why not? _____

_____

How will you represent the unknown number? _____

think
it through

a. To write a variable expression, sometimes it helps to think what you would do if you did have all the information. For example, what operations would you perform to find the total number of pencils if Michelle bought

▶ 1 package? _____

▶ 2 packages? _____

▶ 3 packages? _____

Remember: You can use multiplication to show repeated addition.

essions

answer
the question

The variable expression is _____ .

explain
your answer

I know that Michelle started with _____ pencils. I also know that 1 package of pencils has _____ pencils in it. So, if Michelle buys 1 package of pencils she will be adding 10 pencils to the 3 pencils she already has for a total of _____ pencils. With two packages, Michelle will have $10 + 10 + 3 = 2 \times$ _____ $+ 3 =$ _____ pencils. So, with p packages, Michelle will have $3 +$ _____ pencils.

think
it through

b. You have to find the value of $3 + 10p$ when p is 5. If $p = 5$, Michelle bought 5 packages of pencils.

Write the expression. _____

Substitute 5 for p in the expression. _____

Simplify the expression using the order of operations.

answer
the question

When $p = 5$, the value of the expression is _____.

explain
your answer

If $p = 5$, Michelle bought 5 packages of pencils. I used the expression $3 + 10p$ to calculate the number of pencils Michelle has.

$3 + 10p = 3 + 10 \times 5 = 3 +$ _____ $=$ _____. After purchasing 5 packages, Michelle has 53 pencils.

practice problems: variables and expressions

1. Sofia has 6 bows for decorating birthday presents. She bought more bags of bows. Each bag contains 8 bows.

    a. What variable expression can be used to show the total number of bows Sofia has now? Use b as a variable.

        The expression is _____.

    b. Evaluate the expression if $b = 9$. Explain how you found your answer.

        When $b = 9$, the value of the expression is _____.

2. Justin has to sew 50 stars on a flag. He purchased several packages of stars with 4 stars in each package, but still does not have enough stars.

    a. Write a variable expression to show the number of stars Justin still needs to buy. Use x for the variable.

        The expression is _____.

    b. What does x represent? _____

    c. What does $4x$ represent? _____

3. Sun worked *h* hours in his father's store and *b* hours baby-sitting last week. He earned $5 per hour working in his father's store and $7 an hour baby-sitting.

a. Write an expression showing the total amount Sun earned last week.

The expression is _____.

b. Evaluate the expression if $h = 4$ and $b = 2$. Explain your answer.

4. Veronica bought some red lollipops and some green lollipops. She divided the lollipops into 4 equal groups to give to her friends.

a. Write an expression showing the number of lollipops in each equal group.

The expression is _____.

b. Tell what the variables in your expression represent.

The variable _____ represents _____.

The variable _____ represents _____.

c. How could you write the expression if Veronica bought equal numbers of red and green lollipops? Define your variable(s).

5 **translat**

An **expression** is a mathematical *phrase* that has numbers, operation signs, and sometimes variables. An **equation** is a mathematical *sentence* that shows that two quantities are equal. An equation has an equal sign (=); an expression does not have an equal sign.

problem: A fruit stand sells oranges, apples, and plums. Oranges are $0.75 each, apples are $0.45 each, and the price of plums changes from day to day. Write an expression that could be used to find the total cost of 4 oranges, 6 apples, and 3 plums.

understand
the problem

What is the problem asking you to do? _____

_____

What do you know? _____

think
it through

What does an expression contain? _____

What operations are suggested? _____

How can you represent the unknown price? _____

Write expressions to represent the costs. Use *n* for the variable.

▶ oranges: _____

▶ apples: _____

▶ plums: _____

answer
the question

The total cost of all the fruit = _____

explain
your answer

To find the total cost of the fruit purchased, I added the costs of the oranges, apples, and plums. The oranges cost $4 \times \$$ _____. The apples cost _____ $\times \$0.45$. Because the cost of plums changes from day to day, the cost of plums is $3 \times$ _____ $= 3n$. So, the total cost of the fruit can be shown by the expression $(4 \times \$0.75) + (6 \times \$0.45) + 3n$.

words into expressions and equations

> **problem**: The length of Jarvis's rectangular garden is 3 times the width. The perimeter is 40 meters. Write an equation that could be used to find the length and width of Jarvis's garden.

understand
the problem

What is the problem asking you to do? _____

What do you know about the length? _____

think
it through

How are the length and the width of a rectangle related to its perimeter?

_____

What is the sum of the length and the width of Jarvis's garden? _____

If *w* represents the width, what expression represents the length? _____

Write an expression that represents the sum of the length and the width.

_____

answer
the question

To write an equation that could be used to find the length and width of Jarvis's garden, translate this sentence into an equation.

_____ _____ _____
The sum of the length and the width   is   20.

> **Remember:** The word "is" indicates where to place the equal sign in an equation.

explain
your answer

I know that the _____ is 40 meters, so the

_____ of the length and width is 20 meters. The length is 3

times the width, so I let the variable w represent the _____.

Then, I used the expression 3w to represent the _____. So, the

equation 3w + w = 20 can be used to find the value of w.

1. Ahnah scored 88 points on each of three science exams. On the fourth, exam she scored an unknown number of points, *p*.

a. Write an expression that represents the total number of points Ahnah scored on all four science exams. Explain your reasoning.

b. Ahnah knows that her point total for the four science exams is 354. Write an equation that could be used to find *p*, her unknown score.

2. Travis had a length of rope that was 215 meters long. He used 25 meters of it to tie down some equipment, and he used 75 meters of it to make a perimeter around his garden. Write an equation that could be used to find *r*, the number of meters of rope left over. Explain your reasoning.

3. Wade worked *x* days last semester. Jalleel worked 10 more days than Wade worked.

a. Write an expression for the number of days Jalleel worked.

b. Write an equation that could be used to find the number of days Wade worked if Jaleel worked 25 days.

c. Explain your answers.

4. In football, a team scores 6 points for every touchdown and 3 points for every field goal.

a. Write an expression that could be used to find the total number of points scored by the Tigers football team if the team scored *t* touchdowns and *f* field goals.

b. The Tigers scored 2 field goals in their first game. In that game, they scored a total of 42 points, all on field goals and touchdowns. Write an equation that could be used to find how many touchdowns, *t*, the Tigers scored in that game. Explain your thinking.

Addition problems often use key words such as *sum, plus, more than, total,* and *increased by.* To solve an addition equation, isolate the unknown by subtracting the same number from each side of the equation.

> **problem:** Steve bought a book and a battery-operated light to use when reading the book. The total he paid was $43.50. If the book cost $27.55, how much did he pay for the light? (Assume there was no sales tax.) Explain your answer.

understand
the problem

What is the problem asking you to find? _____

What do you know? _____

think
it through

What operation is suggested? _____

What can be represented by the variable *b?* _____

Write an expression that shows the total cost of the two items. _____

What does the expression equal? _____

Write an addition equation to find the cost of the light. _____

answer
the question

To find the cost of the light, solve the equation for the variable *b.*

> Remember:
> Addition and subtraction
> are inverse operations.

explain
your answer

I know the price of the book. I can represent the unknown value of the light with the variable b to set up the equation $27.55 + b = $_____.
If I subtract $_____ from both sides of the equation, I can solve for the unknown: b = $43.50 − $_____ = $_____.

**ations**

problem: A number increased by 22 equals 87. What is the number?

understand
the problem

What is the problem asking you to find? _____

_____

think
it through

What operation is suggested? How do you know? _____

What is unknown and can be represented by a variable? _____

Write an expression that represents "a number increased by 22." Use the variable *n* to represent the unknown quantity. _____

What should the expression equal? _____

Write an equation that could be used to find the number, *n.* _____

What operation should be used to solve for *n?* _____

answer
the question

To find the number, solve the equation for the variable *n.*

n = _____

explain
your answer

I used the variable n as the unknown value. Because n increased by 22 equals 87, I wrote the equation as n + 22 = _____. Then, I solved for n by subtracting 22 from 87: n = 87 − 22 = _____. The number is _____.

I. Yara studied an unknown number of hours. She practiced the piano for 3 hours. The total number of hours that Yara studied and practiced the piano is 7 hours.

a. Write an equation that could be used to find the unknown number of hours, *s*, that Yara spent studying. Explain your answer.

b. Solve the equation in part a for *s*. Explain how to solve the equation and how to check your answer.

2. The sum of a number and 19 is equal to 45.

a. Write an equation that could be used to find the unknown number, *n*. How did you know what operation to use?

b. Solve the equation in part a for *n*. What operation did you use to solve the equation?

3. Jaime is y years old. In 15 years, he will be 27 years old.

    a. Write an equation that could be used to find Jaime's age now.

    b. Solve the equation for y.

    c. Explain how you got your answer.

4. Four hundred more than j is 801.

    a. Write an equation that could be used to find j.

    b. Solve the equation in part a for j. Show your work.

    c. Is your answer reasonable? How do you know?

7 subtracti

equ

To solve a subtraction equation, add the same number to both sides of the equation. To solve for x in the equation, $x - 7 = 10$, you need to add 7 to both sides of the equation.

> **problem:** Jeanette ate 15 blueberries from a carton. Now, there are 32 blueberries left. How many blueberries were originally in the carton?

understand
the problem

What is the problem asking you to find? _____

What do you know? _____

think
it through

What operation is suggested? _____

What can be represented by a variable? _____

Write an equation to find the difference between the original number of blueberries and the number of blueberries Jeanette ate. Use the variable b.

_____ = 32

What operation should be used to solve for b? _____

answer
the question

To find the number of blueberries originally in the carton, solve the equation for b. Show your work.

> Remember:
> When subtracting, the order of the quantities matters.

$b =$ _____

explain
your answer

I used the variable b as the unknown value. Because 15 blueberries were eaten and there were 32 left, I wrote the equation as b — 15 = _____. I then solved for b by adding 15 to each side of the equation: b = _____ + 15 = _____. There were _____ blueberries in the carton.

ations

problem: A number decreased by 11 equals 26. What is the number?

understand
the problem

What is the problem asking you to find? _____

_____

think
it through

What operation is suggested? How do you know? _____

_____

Write an expression that represents "a number decreased by 11." Use the variable n to represent the unknown number. _____

What should the expression equal? _____

Write an equation that could be used to find the number, n. _____

What operation will you use to solve this equation? _____

answer
the question

Solve the equation for n. Show your work.

$n =$ _____

explain
your answer

I used the variable n as the unknown value. Because n decreased by 11 equals 26, I wrote the equation as $n - 11 =$ _____. Then, I solved for n by adding 11 to both sides: $n = 26 + 11 =$ _____. The number is _____.

practice problems: subtraction equations

1. The difference between a number and 3 is equal to 18.

    a. Write an equation that could be used to find the unknown number, x. Explain how you know what operation to use.

    b. Solve the equation in part a for x. What operation did you use to solve the equation?

2. Kyle jumped 21.25 feet in the long jump competition at a track meet. That length was 2.5 feet shorter than his first jump.

    a. Write an equation that could be used to find the length of Kyle's first jump, j.

    b. Solve the equation in part a for j to find the length, in feet, of Kyle's first jump. Justify your answer.

3. Trina withdrew $70 dollars from her savings account. The new balance in her savings account is $215.

a. Write an equation that could be used to find the amount, w, that Trina started with in her saving account. Explain your answer.

b. Solve the equation in part a for w. Explain how you know your answer is correct.

4. Lily had 21 fewer points during the basketball game than Melissa. Lily scored 16 points.

a. Write an equation that could be used to find the number of points, m, that Melissa scored.

b. Solve the equation in part a for m to find the number of points that Melissa scored. Show your work.

c. Justify your answer.

These are all multiplication equations: $5n = 35$ $5 \times n = 35$ $5(n) = 35$

To solve a multiplication equation, you need to use division. For example, to solve $5n = 35$, you need to divide both sides of the equation by 5.

> **problem:** Alem sold tickets to the school play. The total amount of money he collected was $126.50. The price of each ticket was $5.50. How many tickets did Alem sell? Explain your answer.

> **Remember:**
> Look for these
> key words that indicate
> multiplication: *times, twice,*
> *of, total,* and *product.*

understand
the problem

How much did each ticket cost? _____

How much did Alem collect in all? _____

think
it through

What operation is suggested? _____

Write an expression to find the number of tickets sold. Use the variable *n* to

represent the unknown. _____

What should the expression equal? _____

Write an equation to find the number of tickets sold. _____

What operation will you use to solve this equation? _____

answer
the question

Solve the equation for the variable *n.* Show your work.

Alem sold _____ tickets.

explain
your answer

I know that each ticket cost $5.50 and that Alem had $_____ in total

sales. There were n tickets sold, so I set up an equation to find how many

tickets Alem sold: $5.50(_____) = $126.50. To find n, I divided both sides by

$5.50. n = _____ So, Alem sold 23 tickets.

ations

> **problem**: Inez earns $6.25 per hour baby-sitting. Last week, she earned $31.25. How many hours did she baby-sit last week?

understand
the problem

How much does Inez earn per hour? _____

How much did she earn baby-sitting last week? _____

think
it through

What operation is suggested? _____

What unknown can be represented by a variable? _____

Write an expression that represents the total number of hours Inez baby-sat. Use

the variable n to represent the unknown. _____

What should the expression equal? _____

Write an equation to find the number n. _____

What operation will you use to solve for n in this equation? _____

answer
the question

Solve the equation for the variable n. Show your work.

> Remember:
> Multiplication and division are inverse operations.

Last week, Inez baby-sat for _____ hours.

explain
your answer

To solve the problem, I wrote the equation $6.25n = $31.25. I divided both sides by $6.25 to find that $n = $ _____ hours.

practice problems: multiplication equations

1. During soccer season, Jason scored three times as many goals as Eddie. Jason scored 18 goals.

  a. Write an equation to find the number of goals, g, Eddie scored. Explain your reasoning.

  b. Solve the equation in part a for g to find the number of goals that Eddie scored. Show your work.

  C. Explain how to solve the equation and how to check your answer.

2. The product of a number and 12.62 is 113.58.

  a. Write an equation to find the unknown number, x. Then, explain how you knew what operation to use and where to put the equal sign.

  b. Solve the equation in part a for x. What operation did you use to solve the equation?

3. Forty-four times *y* is 308.

    a. Write an equation that could be used to find *y*. Then, justify your answer.

    b. Solve the equation in part a for *y*. Show your work.

    c. Is your answer reasonable? How do you know?

4. Christie paid twice as much for her new perfume as Nicole. Christie paid $42.

    a. Write an equation that could be used to find the cost of Nicole's perfume, *c*.

    b. Solve the equation in part a for *c* to find the amount that Nicole paid for her perfume. Show your work and check your answer.

These are all division equations: $\frac{x}{3} = 8$ $x \div 3 = 8$ $\frac{1}{3}x = 8$

To solve a division equation, you need to use multiplication. For example, to solve the equation $\frac{x}{3} = 8$, you need to multiply both sides of the equation by 3.

problem: Ben's teacher asked him to separate the pencils in a box into equal groups. Find the number of pencils that are in the box if there are 28 groups of 6 pencils. Justify your answer.

Remember: Look for these key words that indicate division: *per*, *group*, *out of*, and *quotient*.

understand
the problem

What are you trying to find? _____

There are _____ groups of _____ pencils.

think
it through

What operation is suggested? _____

What unknown can be represented by a variable? _____

Write a division expression that can be used to find the number of groups of pencils.

Use the variable *p*. _____

What should the expression equal? _____

The equation is: _____

What operation will you use to solve for *p*? _____

answer
the question

Solve the equation for the variable *p*. Show your work.

There are _____ pencils in the box.

explain
your answer

There are p pencils in the box. I know that the pencils are divided into groups of _____. There are 28 groups. I set up the equation $\frac{p}{6} = 28$. To solve for p, I multiplied both sides of the equation by 6. There are _____ pencils in the box.

ations

> **problem:** Mario's teacher divides the class into 12 equal groups. Each group has 3 students. How many students are in the class?

understand
the problem

What are you trying to find? _____

How many groups are there? _____

How many students are in each group? _____

think
it through

What operation is suggested? _____

What unknown can be represented by a variable? _____

Write a division expression that represents the number of groups. Use the variable

n to represent the unknown quantity. _____

What should the expression equal? _____

Write an equation that can be used to find n. _____

What operation should be used to solve this equation? _____

answer
the question

Solve the equation for the variable n. Show your work.

There are _____ students in the class.

explain
your answer

In a class of n students, there are 12 equal groups of _____ students. I set

up the equation $\frac{n}{3} = 12$ to find how many students are in the class. To solve

the equation, I multiplied both sides of the equation by _____. There are _____

students in the class.

practice problems: division equations

1. Devon and his friends went to a ballgame. They bought nine boxes of popcorn. Each box costs $3.50. How much did they spend on the popcorn in all?

   a. Write a division equation to find the total cost of popcorn, b.

   b. Solve the equation in part a for b to find the total cost of popcorn.

   c. Explain how to check your answer.

2. Maria equally divided her knitting yarn into 7 bins. She put 8 balls of yarn in each bin. How many balls of yarn does she have?

   a. Write a division equation to find the total number of balls of yarn, y.

   b. Solve the equation in part a for y to find the total number of balls of yarn. Explain how to check your answer.

3. A number divided by 220 is 14.

a. Write a division equation to find the number. Use the variable z for the unknown quantity. Then, explain your answer.

b. Solve the equation in part a for z. Show your work. Is your answer reasonable? How do you know?

4. Aaron drove to visit his grandmother. He drove 62 miles per hour for 16 hours.

a. Write a division equation to find the total number of miles, m, that Aaron drove.

b. Solve the equation in part a for m to find the number of miles that Aaron drove. Show your work and check your answer.

10

ratio

A **ratio** is a comparison of two quantities or numbers. The ratio comparing *a* to *b* can be written as $\frac{a}{b}$, *a:b,* or *a* to *b* (*b* is a nonzero number). The words *compare* and *comparison* are signs that a problem requires a ratio.

problem: The table shows the sightings of different birds at a state park.

Birds Sighted March 11–17				
Type of Bird	Marten	Wren	Woodpecker	Owl
Number Seen	8	15	6	2

a. Write a ratio comparing the number of owls seen to the number of woodpeckers seen. Then write a ratio comparing the number of wrens seen to the number of martens seen. Explain your reasoning.

b. Which ratio is greater? Explain your answer.

understand
the problem

What does the first ratio compare? _____

What does the second ratio compare? _____

How can you decide which ratio is larger? _____

_____

think
it through

a. How many owls were seen? _____

How many woodpeckers were seen? _____

How many wrens were seen? _____

How many martens were seen? _____

answer
the question

The ratio of owl sightings to woodpecker sightings is _____.

The ratio of wren sightings to marten sightings is _____.

explain
your answer

There were _____ owls seen and _____ woodpeckers seen. The ratio of owl sightings to woodpecker sightings is _____, which can be simplified. In simplest terms, $\frac{2}{6}$ is equal to _____.

There were _____ wrens seen and _____ martens seen. The ratio of wren sightings to marten sightings is _____ .

think
it through

b. Compare the two ratios.

$\frac{1}{3} \approx 0.33$, which is less than one. $0.33 < 1.00$.

$\frac{15}{8} = 1.875$, which is more than one. $1.875 > 1.00$.

Therefore, _____ is greater than _____.

_____ > _____

answer
the question

Which ratio is greater? _____

explain
your answer

To find which ratio is greater, I wrote each as a decimal:

$\frac{1}{3} =$ _____ and $\frac{15}{8} =$ _____

1.875 is greater than _____, so $\frac{15}{8}$ is _____ than $\frac{1}{3}$.

Remember: The order of quantities in a ratio matters. Be sure to use the order asked for in the problem.

1. A recipe for fruit punch calls for 16 ounces of orange juice, 12 ounces of lemonade, and 46 ounces of unsweetened pineapple juice.

a. Write the ratio of orange juice to lemonade using a fraction in its simplest form. Simplify your answer. Show your work.

b. Write the ratio of lemonade to unsweetened pineapple juice in the form a:b.

2. Zoe, Meghan, and Fumi used ratios to describe a CD they made containing 8 country songs and 9 pop rock songs.

Zoe $\frac{8}{9}$ Meghan 9:8   Fumi $\frac{9}{17}$

Explain how each girl's ratio could be correct.

3. In a group of 30, the ratio of item A to item B is 2:3. The ratio of A to B is supposed to be 1:1. How many As need to be added to the group for the ratio of A to B to be 1:1? Explain your answer.

4. In a jar, there are 8 black buttons, 6 shell buttons, 11 white buttons, and 5 metal buttons. Would the following ratios change if three shell buttons are added to the jar? Explain why or why not.

▶ the ratio of white buttons to black buttons

▶ the ratio of metal buttons to total buttons

▶ the ratio of shell buttons to metal buttons

After the shell buttons are added, what is the ratio of metal buttons to total buttons?

rate

A **rate** is a ratio that compares different units of measurement, like miles per hour or feet per second. A unit rate has a denominator of 1. Some examples of unit rates are 4 people per car, 12 inches per foot, or $1.50 per pound.

problem: As a part of his exercise program, Chung aims to reach a target heart rate of 160 beats per minute. During one workout, his heart beat 75 times in 30 seconds.

a. Is Chung exercising above or below his target heart rate?

b. If his resting heart rate is 65 beats per minute, what is the difference between his resting heart rate and his heart rate while exercising?

understand
the problem

What is Chung's target heart rate? _____

While exercising, his heart beat _____ times in _____ seconds.

There are _____ seconds in 1 minute.

think
it through

a. You know that Chung's heart beat _____ times in 30 seconds. And

you know that there are _____ seconds in one minute.

So, if 30 seconds × _____ = 1 minute, then

75 beats × _____ = _____ beats per minute.

Target heart rate is: _____ beats per minute

Heart rate while exercising is: _____ beats per minute

Now, compare the rates.

_____ < _____

Remember: To compare two rates, both rates must use the same units of measurement.

answer
the question

Chung is exercising _____ his target heart rate.

explain
your answer

While exercising, Chung's heart beat _____ times in 30 seconds. There are 60 seconds in 1 minute, so I multiplied 75 × _____ to find Chung's heart rate in beats per minute. Because 150 < 160, Chung is exercising _____ his target heart rate.

think
it through

b. Chung's heart rate while exercising is _____ beats per minute.

His resting heart rate is _____ per minute.

What operation do you use to find the difference between the two rates?

_____

Heart rate after exercising – Resting heart rate

_____ – _____

_____ – _____ = _____

answer
the question

The difference between Chung's heart rate after exercising and his resting rate is _____ beats per minute.

explain
your answer

To find the difference between Chung's heart rate during exercise and his resting heart rate, I used subtraction. I subtracted _____ beats from 150 beats to get a difference of _____ beats per minute.

1. Ava is training for a bike race. Her target racing speed is 25 miles per hour. On her last day of training, she rode 14 miles in 30 minutes.

a. Was her speed on her last day above or below her target racing speed? Explain.

Her training speed is _____ her target racing speed.

b. Heather is training for the same bike race. During training, Heather rode 3 miles in 10 minutes. Who is faster, Ava or Heather? Show your work and explain how you found your answer.

_____ is faster.

c. Last year's bike race winner had an average speed of 27 miles per hour. How much will Heather have to increase her speed to beat last year's winner? Show your work or explain how you found your answer.

2. It takes Mary 30 minutes to walk 2 miles to school. If she biked to school, it would take her 10 minutes.

a. How many miles per hour does Mary walk?

b. What is the difference per hour between her biking rate and her walking rate? Explain your answer.

3. Malcolm can read 35 pages in 20 minutes. He needs to finish a 240-page book in 3 hours. At his reading rate, will he be able to finish reading his book? Explain your answer.

12

A **proportion** is an equation that shows equivalent ratios. For example, the proportion $\frac{3}{4} = \frac{6}{8}$ shows that the ratio $\frac{3}{4}$ is equivalent to the ratio $\frac{6}{8}$. Proportions that contain a variable can be solved by using cross products.

> **problem**: An inkjet printer can print 5 pages in 15 seconds. How many minutes will it take for the printer to print 120 pages? Explain how to solve the problem. Then solve the problem.

understand
the problem

What are you asked to find? _____

_____

What is the speed of the printer? _____

Will the answer be in seconds or minutes? _____

think
it through

First identify the unknown in the problem. Use the variable x to represent the unknown. What will x represent? _____

_____

You can solve the problem by using a proportion. Your answer will be in seconds, but you need to find the number of minutes. How will you convert the answer to minutes? _____

answer
the question

Write a proportion that compares the number of pages printed to the time it takes to print them. You are comparing printed pages to time, so the number of pages will be in the numerator of each ratio and the time will be in the denominator.

> **Remember:**
> The problem asks for the answer in minutes, so you need to convert pages per second to pages per minute.

ortions

$$\frac{\text{number of pages}}{\text{time}} = \frac{\text{number of pages}}{\text{time}}$$

$$\frac{5}{\rule{1cm}{0.4pt}} = \frac{120}{\rule{1cm}{0.4pt}}$$

Use cross products to solve for the variable

$$\frac{5}{15} \diagdown\!\!\!\!\diagup \frac{120}{x}$$

Write the equation and solve for x.

$x =$ _____ seconds

Convert the number of seconds to minutes by _____.

360 ___ _____ = _____

The printer can print 120 pages in _____ minutes.

explain
your answer

I know that the printer will print 5 pages in _____ seconds, which can be expressed as the ratio _____. I used the variable x to represent the number of seconds it will take to print 120 pages. I then set up and solved a proportion to find that it will take 360 seconds to print 120 pages. There are 60 seconds in 1 minute, so it will take 360 ÷ 60 or _____ minutes to print 120 pages.

1. A 4-fluid-ounce glass of orange juice contains 50 calories. How many calories are in 2 cups of orange juice?

a. Explain how to solve the problem.

b. Solve the problem. Show your work.

2. A Ferris wheel makes two revolutions in 30 seconds. A ride on the Ferris wheel takes $2\frac{1}{2}$ minutes. How many times does the Ferris wheel revolve during the ride?

a. Explain how to solve the problem.

b. Solve the problem. Show your work.

3. Dana bought a 32-pound bag of dog food. Her dog eats 4 ounces of dog food at each meal. If her dog eats twice a day, how many days will the bag of food last?

a. Explain how to solve the problem.

b. Solve the problem. Show your work.

4. Jake walks 3.5 miles in 50 minutes. At the same rate of speed, how far can Jake walk in 2 hours and 30 minutes?

a. Write a proportion to solve the problem. Explain how you arrived at your answer.

b. Use the proportion you wrote in part a to solve the problem. Show your work.

13 similar Fig

Similar figures have the same shape but are not necessarily the same size. The corresponding angles of similar figures are congruent. The lengths of the corresponding sides of similar figures are proportional.

problem: Janelle has a doghouse for her dog, Cleo. She wants to build a separate doghouse for her new puppy, Duncan. Janelle wants the doghouses to be similar in shape. She decides the length of Duncan's doghouse will be 36 inches. How wide should Duncan's doghouse be? Explain how to solve the problem. Then, solve the problem.

$w = 20$ in.

Cleo's Doghouse

$l = 48$ in.

understand
the problem

What are you asked to find? _____

What are the dimensions of Cleo's doghouse? _____

What do you know about the dimensions of Duncan's doghouse? _____

_____

think
it through

First identify the unknown in the problem. Use the variable w to represent the

unknown. What does w represent? _____

$w = 20$ in. | **Cleo's Doghouse**

$l = 48$ in.

$w = ?$ | **Duncan's Doghouse**

$l = 36$ in.

You can find the width of this similar figure using _____

ures

answer the question

You know that the two doghouses are similar in shape. Use what you know about similar figures to decide how to solve the problem.

Because the bases are similar, you can write a proportion that compares the corresponding dimensions of the bases. Then, use the cross products to solve for the variable.

Complete the proportions.

$$\frac{\text{Cleo's doghouse}}{\text{Duncan's doghouse}} \blacktriangleright \quad \frac{\text{width}}{\text{width}} = \frac{\text{length}}{\text{length}}$$

$$\frac{\text{Cleo's doghouse}}{\text{Duncan's doghouse}} \blacktriangleright \quad \frac{20}{\rule{1cm}{0.4pt}} = \frac{48}{\rule{1cm}{0.4pt}}$$

Use the cross products to solve for the variable.

$$\frac{20}{w} \diagdown\!\!\!\diagup \frac{48}{36}$$

Write the equation and solve for w.

Duncan's doghouse should be _____ inches wide.

explain your answer

Because the two doghouses are similar in shape, you can write a proportion to compare the lengths and widths of the two doghouses: $\frac{20}{w} = \frac{48}{36}$. The variable w represents the width of Duncan's doghouse. Then, cross-multiply to get the equation 48 _____ = 20 × 36. Next, multiply 20 × 36, and then divide both sides of the equation by _____ to get w = _____.

1. Jackie knitted a placemat 15 inches long by 12 inches wide. She wants to knit a potholder that is similar in shape to the placemat. Jackie wants the potholder to be 4 inches wide. What should the length of the potholder be?

a. Write a proportion that can be used to solve the problem. Explain your proportion.

b. Use the proportion you wrote to solve the problem. Show your work.

2. The dimensions of two windows are shown below.

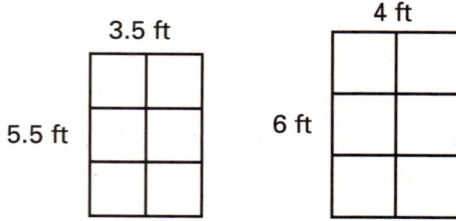

Are the windows similar? Explain why or why not. Show your work to justify your answer.

3. Marco wants to make a large triangular banner that is similar in shape to a small triangular banner. The dimensions of each banner are shown below. What is the value of *x*, in centimeters?

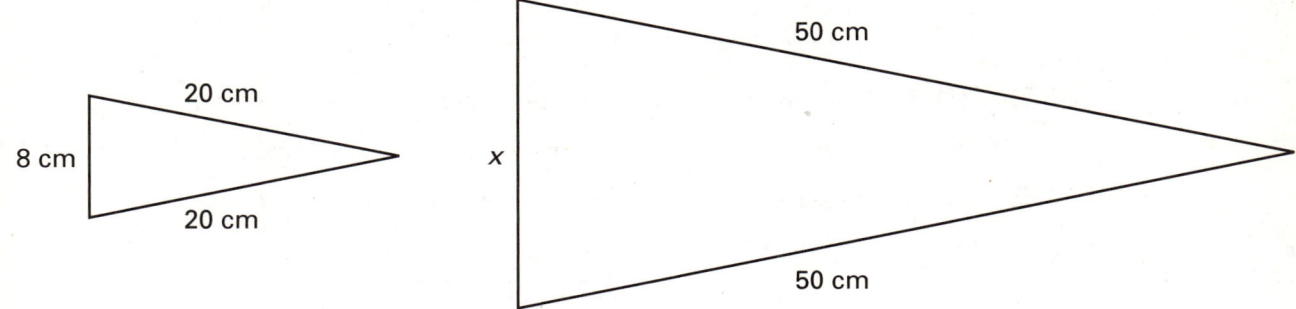

a. Explain how to solve the problem.

b. Solve the problem. Show your work.

The dimensions of a **scale drawing** are in proportion to the actual dimensions of the object. A **map** is an example of a scale drawing. If a map is drawn to a scale of 1 inch = 100 miles, then cities 2 inches apart on the map are actually 200 miles apart.

problem: Nasir made a scale drawing of the floor plan for a rectangular house. The house is 40 feet long and 25 feet wide.

a. On his scale drawing, the house is 5 inches wide. What scale did Nasir use?

b. The lot that the house is on is 100 feet long and 40 feet wide. Suppose Nasir used the same dimensions for a scale drawing showing the entire lot. What would the length and width of the lot be on the drawing? Justify your answer.

understand
the problem

What are the dimensions of the actual house? _____

The house is measured in feet. What units are used to measure the scale drawing?

_____

think
it through

a. What scale did Nasir use in his scale drawing? You can use a proportion to determine the scale. A drawing can help you see the proportion.

```
┌─────────────────────┐
│                     │
│                     │
│      actual         │  25 ft       ┌──────────┐
│                     │              │  scale   │  5 in
│                     │              │  model   │
└─────────────────────┘              └──────────┘
        40 ft
```

What is the actual width of the house? _____ feet

What is the width of the house in the scale drawing? _____ inches

Set up a ratio with the two widths. Reduce the ratio to its simplest terms to find the scale.

$$\frac{\_\_\_\ \text{feet}}{5\ \text{inches}} = \frac{\_\_\_\ \text{feet}}{\_\_\_\ \text{inch}}$$

gs and
maps

answer
the question

What scale did Nasir use in his drawing? 1 inch : _____ feet

explain
your answer

The width of the house is _____ feet and the width of the model is _____ inches. I can write a ratio to find the scale of the drawing: $\frac{25 \text{ feet}}{5 \text{ inches}}$. I simplified the fraction as _____. The scale of the model is 1 inch = _____ feet.

think
it through

b. The actual length of the lot is 100 feet. Set up a proportion to find the length in the scale drawing. Compare the scale factor to the lot length.

$$\frac{5 \text{ feet}}{1 \text{ inch}} = \frac{}{x \text{ inches}}$$

Set up a proportion to find the width in the scale drawing.

answer
the question

Solve each proportion.

Proportion to find length	Proportion to find width

The lot is _____ inches long and _____ inches wide on the scale drawing.

explain
your answer

I used the scale factor from part a to figure out the length and width of the lot.

1 inch : _____ feet is the same as _____ inches : 100 feet. The length of the lot in the drawing is _____ inches.

1 inch : 5 feet is the same as 8 inches : _____ feet. The width of the lot in the drawing is _____ inches.

I. Rick made a scale drawing of a rectangular vegetable garden. The actual garden is 6 meters long and 4 meters wide. In the scale drawing, the garden is 2 centimeters wide.

a. What scale did Rick use?

b. How long is the garden in the scale drawing?

c. Rick wants to expand his vegetable garden to be 10 meters wide and 15 meters long. Using the same scale, what are the dimensions of the expanded garden in a scale drawing? Explain how you found your answer.

2. An artist made a scale drawing of a large rectangular painting. The actual painting is 15 meters long and 8 meters wide.

a. If the scale is 1 centimeter = 4 meters, what are the dimensions of the painting in the scale drawing? Show your work.

b. If the scale drawing showed the length to be 3 cm long, what scale was used to make the drawing? Explain your answer.

3. Northport Elementary is holding a contest for students to design a new mural for the cafeteria. The final rectangular-shaped mural will measure 60 inches by 40 inches. The art teacher wants to design a scale outline of the mural that is no larger than 7 inches wide and 9 inches long so that it will fit on copy paper for student entries.

a. What is the largest scale factor that can be used? Show your work.

b. Using the scale factor in part a, what will be the actual dimensions of the scale for student entries?

A **percent** is a ratio that compares a number to 100. The percent sign (%) means *parts per hundred*. A percent can be expressed as a fraction or as a decimal. For example, 25% can be written as $\frac{25}{100}$ or 0.25.

problem: The season home run records for Raul, Tom, and David are shown in the table. For each player, find the percentage of hits that were home runs.

Season Record		
	Home Runs	**Total Hits**
Raul	4	25
Tom	6	30
David	3	10

understand
the problem

Look at how many home runs and hits each player had.

Raul: _____ home runs and _____ total hits

Tom: _____ home runs and _____ total hits

David: _____ home runs and _____ total hits

think
it through

To find the percentages, first write each player's hits as a ratio of home runs to total hits.

Raul: _____   Tom: _____   David: _____

Percent means "per hundred" so the denominator of each fraction needs to be _____.

For Raul and David, the denominators are factors of 100. So, for each fraction, write an equivalent fraction with 100 as the denominator.

decimals, and
tables

Raul: $\frac{4}{25} = \frac{x}{100}$ David: $\frac{3}{10} = \frac{x}{100}$

What number times 25 is equal to 100? _____

What number times 10 is equal to 100? _____

Raul: $\frac{4 \times }{25 \times } = \frac{x}{100}$ David: $\frac{3 \times }{10 \times } = \frac{x}{100}$

$\frac{4}{25} = \frac{16}{100}$ $\frac{3}{10} = \frac{30}{100}$

For Tom, the denominator is not a factor of 100.

To find Tom's percentage, convert $\frac{6}{30}$ to a decimal.

Divide 6 by 30. $\frac{6}{30} = $ _____.

Then, convert the decimal to a percent by multiplying by 100.

> **Remember:** To change a fraction to a percent, first divide the numerator by the denominator. Then, move the decimal point 2 places to the right and add a % sign.

answer
the question

The percentage of home runs Raul hit is _____%.

The percentage of home runs Tom hit is _____%.

The percentage of home runs David hit is _____%.

explain
your answer

To find the percents, I first wrote each ratio of home runs to total hits as a fraction. For Raul and David, the fractions had denominators that are factors of _____, so I found the percents by rewriting the fractions with denominators of 100. For Tom, the denominator is not a factor of 100, so I converted it to a decimal and multiplied by _____.

1. Four out of five students went on a field trip. What percentage of students went on the field trip? Explain your answer.

2. A portion of this circle is shaded.

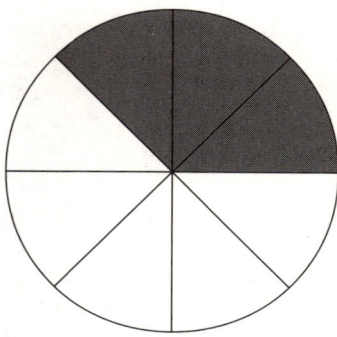

   a. Describe the shaded portion of the circle as a fraction, a decimal, and a percent.

   b. Now describe the *unshaded* portion of the circle as a fraction, a decimal, and a percent.

3. A U.S. coin represents a certain percent of one dollar. A quarter is worth $0.25, a dime is worth $0.10, a nickel is worth $0.05, and a penny is worth $0.01. Express the value of each coin as a percent and as a fraction of a dollar. Write the fractions in simplest terms.

4. In England before 1971, the currency was not based on a decimal system. The table shows several old coins and their values.

English Currency before Decimalization	
Coin	**Value**
farthing	$\frac{1}{4}$ penny
tuppence	2 pence
shilling	12 pence
half crown	2 shillings 6 pence
pound	20 shillings

a. Express the value of a shilling as a percent of a pound. Justify your answer.

b. Express a half crown as a fraction of a pound. Justify your answer.

pe

A **percent** is a ratio whose denominator is 100. Percent means parts per hundred. 5% can be written as the ratio $\frac{5}{100}$ or as the decimal 0.05. Most percent problems can be solved by writing an equation.

> **problem:** Justine is buying a sweater on sale for 20% off of the original price. The sale price of the sweater is $32. Write an equation that will determine the original price of the sweater, *p*. Then find the original price.

understand
the problem

By what percent is the original price reduced? _____

The sale price is _____% of the original price.

think
it through

What do you know about the price of the sweater? _____

_____

What are you trying to find? _____

Translate the following sentence into an equation using *p* as the variable.
The sale price is 80% of the regular price.

_____

answer
the question

To find the original price, solve the equation for *p*. Show your work.

explain
your answer

Because Justine's sweater was reduced by 20%, she paid _____% of the original price. I set up this equation: $32 = _____ × p. To calculate the original price of the sweater, p, I used division. The original price of the sweater is $_____.

problem: A class poll was taken to find out students' favorite sports. The results are shown on the pie chart. Thirty-six students voted for football. What is the total number of students who voted?

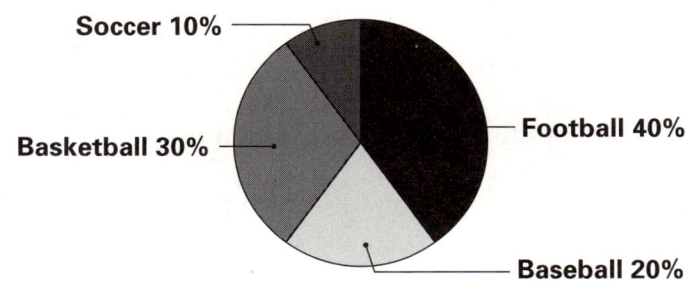

Soccer 10%

Basketball 30%

Football 40%

Baseball 20%

understand
the problem

How many students voted for football? _____

What percent of students voted for football? _____ baseball? _____ basketball? _____

think
it through

What do you know? _____

What are you trying to find? _____

Translate the following sentence into an equation using *s* as the variable.

36 is 40% of the total number of students. _____

What operation will you use to solve the equation? _____

answer
the question

To find out how many students voted, solve the equation for *s.*

explain
your answer

The 36 students who voted for football represent _____% of the total

students who voted. I set up the equation: 36 = _____ × s, to solve for the

total number of students. Then, I divided both sides of the equation by 0.40 to

get: _____ students voted.

1. Carlos purchased a new video game console that was 40% off of the original price. He paid $72 for the game console, without tax.

   a. Write an equation to find the cost, *c*, of the game console before the discount.

   b. What is the original price of the game console? Explain how you found your answer.

2. Melanie is also thinking of buying a video game console that is being reduced from $110 to $88. Write and solve an equation to find the discount rate as a percent.

3. Jamila sold 36 tickets to a junior prom. She sold 20% of the total number of tickets that were sold. Write and solve an equation to determine how many tickets were sold altogether. Let n be the total number of tickets sold. Describe how you found your answer.

4. A lamp is on sale for 25% off of the original price of $36. Joanne receives an employee discount of 10% off all merchandise. If an item is already on sale, employees get 10% off the sale price of the item.

a. Write and solve an equation that determines what Joanne will pay after the two discounts. Explain your reasoning.

b. Is this price the same as receiving a 35% discount on the lamp? Explain your answer.

17 **more app**

pe

To write a percent as a ratio in fraction form, first drop the percent sign. Then, write the number as a numerator with a denominator of 100. For example, $15\% = \frac{15}{100}$

problem: Anthony purchased a car in 2006. A year later, the car is worth only 74% of its original price. It is worth $15,540. Write and solve a proportion to determine the original price of the car. Show your work.

understand
the problem

How much is the car worth now? _____

The current value of the car is _____% of the car's original price.

think
it through

Compare the current value to the original price.

$$\frac{\% \text{ of original price}}{100} = \frac{\text{value after 1 year}}{\text{original price of car}}$$

Fill in the information you know using n for the unknown.

$$\frac{}{100} = \frac{}{}$$

answer
the question

Solve using cross products.

Remember:
A proportion is an equation that shows two equivalent ratios.

$n =$ _____

explain
your answer

I wrote a proportion to compare 74% (or $\frac{74}{100}$) to the ratio of the current value of the car over the original price of the car. I let n represent the original price of the car. I cross-multiplied, and solved for n. The original price of the car was $_____.

problem: Melinda bought a baseball trading card for $25 last year. This year, the trading card is valued at $28. If the trading card continues to increase in value by the same percent, what will it be worth a year from now? Explain.

understand
the problem

What is the original price of the trading card? _____

How much is the trading card worth now? _____

What is the difference between the value last year and this year? _____

think
it through

Write and solve a proportion to find the rate of increase.

$$\frac{}{25} = \frac{p}{100}$$

$$25p = \boxed{} \times 100$$

$$p = \boxed{}$$

Remember:
Compare the change
in value to the original value
to find the percent of
increase.

What is the value of the trading card this year? _____

Find the change in the value of the trading card after another year.

$$28 \times \boxed{}\% = 28 \times \boxed{} = \boxed{}$$

answer
the question

Add the change to the current value of the trading card.

$28 + $ _____ = $ _____

explain
your answer

Because the card increased in value by $_____, I calculated the percent change to be $\frac{3}{25}$ or _____%. To find the value of the card next year, I figured out 12% of the card's current value = $_____. Then, I added that to the current value to get a total of $_____.

I. Martina made a donation of 9% of the money she earned this summer to her local SPCA. She donated $139.

a. Write a proportion to determine the amount of money she earned using n for the variable.

b. How much did Martina make this summer? Show your work.

Martina earned _____ this summer.

2. A new motor oil makes vehicles run more efficiently and use 5% less gasoline. Simon drove 22,400 miles last year and averaged 28 miles per gallon. Write and solve a proportion to determine the amount of gas Simon could have saved last year if he had used the new motor oil. Let g be the number of gallons saved. Explain your answer.

3. During a basketball game between Eastern and Western High Schools, a technical foul is called on Eastern. The coach of Western can send any player to the foul line to shoot the free throws. She wants to select the player with the best percentage of made free throws. Which player should the coach select? Use mathematics to justify your response.

Player	Shots attempted	Shots made
Lauren	30	17
Cassidy	20	12
Brogan	19	11
Jessica	16	9

4. Samin owns a retail store. The basic floor plan of his store is shown below. He wants to alter the floor plan so that he can add more merchandise. He needs to use 60% of the total area for floor space. He cannot add onto the building, so he must reduce the size of the work and storage spaces.

```
+---------------------+----------------------+
|                     |   Work space         |
|                     |   300 ft²            |
|   Floor space       +----------------------+
|   800 ft²           |                      |
|                     |   Storage space      |
|                     |   500 ft²            |
+---------------------+----------------------+
```

a. Determine what percentage of the total area of Samin's store is currently floor space. Use mathematics to justify your response.

b. Samin can only reduce his storage space by 100 ft². How much additional space must be reduced from the work space for him to have 60% floor space? Use mathematics to justify your response.

Patterns are found in a sequence of numbers when there is a common difference between the terms. If you can find the pattern, then you can predict other numbers in a sequence.

problem: Thuyen is raising money for her 6th grade class by selling fruit baskets. The table shows how much her class profits based on the number of baskets sold.

Number of Fruit Baskets	Profit (in dollars)
3	36
4	48
5	60
6	72
7	?
12	?

a. Write an equation that can be used to find the profit for any number of baskets sold. Then, complete the table.

b. How many fruit baskets must be sold for the school to earn a $500 profit? Explain your answer.

understand
the problem

You have to find the relationship between the number of fruit baskets sold and the profit earned. Look for a pattern in the table.

think
it through

a. To determine how much the profit increases for each basket sold, you can subtract two consecutive values. This is called finding a common difference. What is the difference between:

36 and 48? _____ 48 and 60? _____ 60 and 72? _____

The common difference is _____.

Now you can multiply the common difference by any number of baskets sold to find the profit earned.

What is the profit earned if x fruit baskets are sold?

x fruit baskets × _____ dollars = _____ dollars profit

What is the profit for 7 baskets? _____

What is the profit for 12 baskets? _____

patterns, and tables

answer
the question

Let x = the number of baskets sold. Let y = the profit in dollars.

The equation is _____.

The profit earned for 7 fruit baskets is _____.

The profit earned for 12 fruit baskets is _____.

explain
your answer

To write the equation, I looked for a common _____ between the profits earned. I found that the common difference is _____, so the profit for each basket is \$12. If x = the number of baskets sold and y = the profit in dollars, then y = _____.

think
it through

b. Use the equation from part a to find the number of baskets that will produce a \$500 profit. The y-variable represents profit, so substitute 500 for y.

_____ = 12x

$\frac{500}{12} = \frac{12x}{12}$ ◀ solve for x by dividing both sides by 12

$41\frac{2}{3} = x$

$x \approx$ _____ ◀ round up to ensure a \$500 profit

Remember:
The answer must
be a whole
number.

answer
the question

To produce \$500 profit, _____ baskets need to be sold.

explain
your answer

I used the equation y = 12x. Because y represents the profit earned, I let y = _____. Then I solved for x to find the number of baskets. The answer was not a whole number. Only whole baskets can be sold, so I checked the profits for 41 baskets and 42 baskets. The profit for 41 baskets is only \$ _____. For 42 baskets, the profit is \$ _____. So, _____ baskets need to be sold.

practice problems: functions, patterns, and tables

1. Spencer earns $7.50 per hour.

a. Write an equation that shows the relationship between h, the number of hours Spencer works, and d, the number of dollars he earns.

The equation is _____.

b. If Spencer receives a paycheck in the amount of $150, how many hours did he work during that pay period? Show your work.

Spencer worked _____ hours.

2. Mikaela deposits the same amount into a bank account each week. The table shows how much is in her account at the end of each week.

Week	Balance (in dollars)
5	75
6	90
7	105
8	120

a. Write an equation that can be used to find the amount in Mikaela's account for any week. Let w = the number of weeks and b = the amount in her account. Explain your reasoning.

b. Mikaela needs to save $380 to go on a school trip. How many weeks will it take her to save the money? Explain how you found your answer.

3. Chloe's parents opened a no-interest savings account for her. They made an initial deposit. Now, every week, Chloe deposits a certain amount into the account. The following table shows her weekly statements. How much did Chloe's parents initially deposit into her account? Use mathematics to justify your response.

Number of weeks	Savings account balance
1	125
2	150
3	175
4	200
5	225

4. A parachutist opens his parachute at a height of 600 feet and descends to the ground at a rate of 5 feet per second. The table below tracks his height over time.

Time (in seconds)	Height (in feet)
0	600
1	595
2	590
3	585

a. Let t = the number of seconds and h = the height, in feet, of the parachutist. Write an equation that will determine the height of the parachutist after any number of seconds. Explain your answer.

b. What will be the height of the parachutist after 8 seconds?

Graphs can show the relationship between two variables, like distance traveled over time, or cost compared to number of units sold. You can use graphs to answer questions about a certain data point, or to help predict an unknown value. You can write equations to describe graphs.

problem: A tour bus travels a certain number of miles in a given day. The graph below represents the relationship between number of days and total miles traveled.

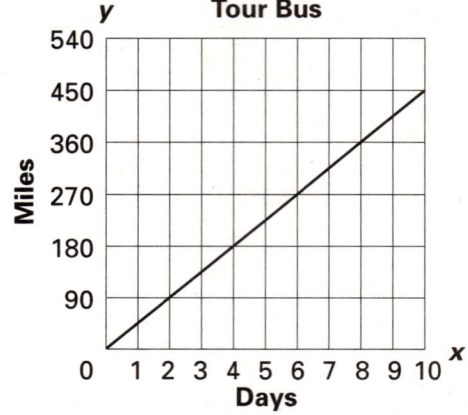

a. How many miles does the bus travel in 2 days? How many miles does it travel in 4 days? Write an equation that shows x number of days and y total miles traveled.

b. Use the graph to predict how many days it would take the bus to travel 945 miles. Use your equation from part a to justify your response.

understand
the problem

What two variables are shown on the graph? _____

Which axis represents the number of days? _____

Which axis represents the number of miles traveled? _____

think
it through

a. Look on the x-axis for 2 days, and find the corresponding y point on the graph.

How many miles does the bus travel in 2 days? _____

Look on the x-axis for 4 days, and find the corresponding y point on the graph.

How many miles can the bus travel after 4 days? _____

nctions

Because the graph is a straight line, you can write an equation relating the total miles traveled (*y*) and the number of days traveled (*x*). Look for a pattern.

- ▶ 2 days   90 miles = 45 × 2
- ▶ 4 days   180 miles = 45 × 4
- ▶ 6 days   270 miles = 45 × 6
- ▶ *x* days   45*x* miles = 45 × *x*

answer
the question

The equation is _____

explain
your answer

Looking at the graph, I saw that the bus traveled _____ miles in 2 days. It traveled _____ miles in 4 days. There is a pattern between the number of days the bus traveled and the total distance it traveled. If y represents the total miles traveled and x is the number of days traveled, I can express the pattern with the equation _____.

think
it through

b. Recall that each day adds an additional 45 miles to the total. Guess and check. The bus can travel 450 miles in 10 days. It can travel 4,500 miles in 100 days. Try other values for *x* greater than 10, but much less than 100.

Solve algebraically.

answer
the question

It will take the bus _____ days to travel 945 miles.

explain
your answer

If it takes 10 days to travel 450 miles, it will take _____ days to travel 900 miles. It takes _____ day to travel 45 miles so it would take _____ days to travel 945 miles. I can justify my answer by substituting 21 for y in the equation: 945 = 45x. 945 ÷ 45 = 21.

I. The senior class charges the same price for each prom ticket. The graph below represents the amount of money that the senior class raised from selling tickets.

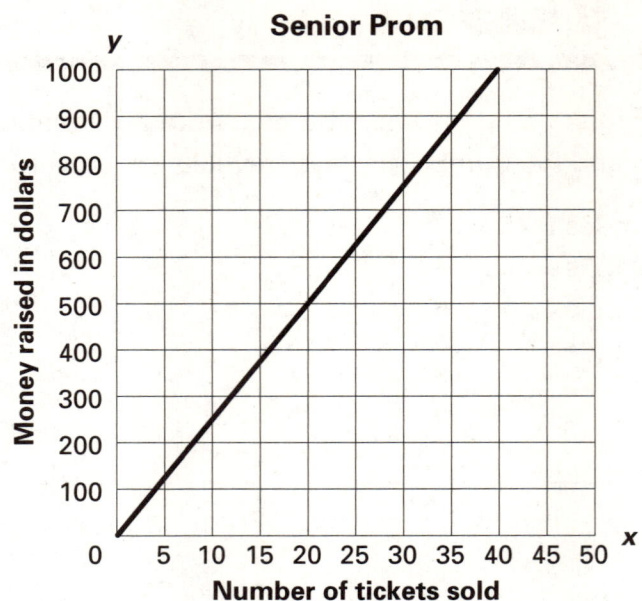

Senior Prom

Money raised in dollars (y-axis: 100, 200, 300, 400, 500, 600, 700, 800, 900, 1000)

Number of tickets sold (x-axis: 5, 10, 15, 20, 25, 30, 35, 40, 45, 50)

a. How much does the senior class charge for each ticket? Use this information to write an equation using *x* for the number of tickets sold and *y* for the amount of money raised.

b. How much would the senior class raise if it sold 200 tickets? Use the equation from part a to justify your response.

c. How would the equation from part b change if the school charged the class a one-time $300 clean-up fee? How would the graph look now? Explain your answer.

2. Matthew has $360 with which he wants to purchase CDs and DVDs from a local electronic store. The following graph represents the number of CDs and DVDs he can purchase for $360. For example, he can buy 8 CDs and 24 DVDs. All CDs cost $9 each. The cost of each DVD is the same.

If Matthew buys 24 CDs, how many DVDs can he purchase? Use your answer to determine the cost of one DVD. Let x be the cost of a DVD. Show your work.

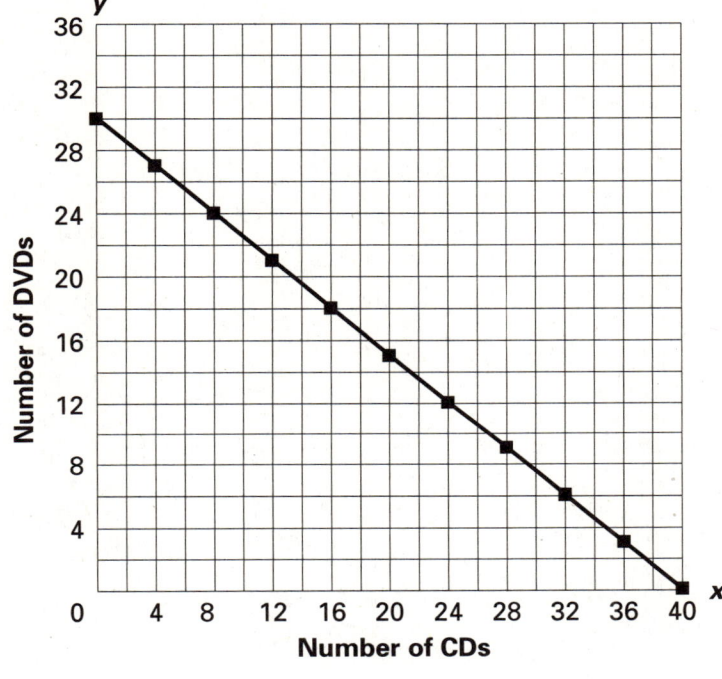